To: Cora

For this God is our God
for ever and ever: he will be
our guide even unto death.
Psalm 48: 14.

May God's favor be
on you always.

Pauline Salmon

Aug 2015

Renting From The Bank

Finding strength in God to triumph over our trials

Dr. Pauline Salmon

Published by

Rays Of Light International, LLC

Spokane, WA

Book and cover design by Rays Of Light International, LLC
Author's photograph by Leslie Francis

Printed in the United States of America.

Unless otherwise noted, all Scriptures are taken from the Holy
Bible, Kings James Version.

ISBN-13: **978-1512156409**
ISBN-10: **151215640X**

First Edition: May 2015

DEDICATION

To my family and friends

TABLE OF CONTENTS

INTRODUCTION

In this business of life, we never know what kind of wind will blow for us. Will it be a balmy, gentle breeze? Will it reach gale force proportions, a storm, or even a hurricane? What we do know is that our heavenly Father is the One who walked on the water and spoke to the wind and the waves and they obeyed Him. We know too, that He being infinite, knows the beginning from the end. As each storm assails us, He is the one who can best judge, decide and move on our behalf. Because of His love and through faith in his promises, we know He will either stop the storm or hold our hand as He sees us through. To our finite minds, answers which may seem to make sense are not necessarily the right ones. People may be well-meaning and may offer advice; advice which often confuse. What can we rely on? *The peace of God which passes understanding* (Phil. 4:7), is one sure way to know that we are walking in God's will. Know that peace when it comes. It is an unnatural peace; it is a supernatural peace.

The summer started out like many others. But this might have been a sign. A pastor once said in his message, that "the only difference between a rut and a grave is the depth." It seems that I was in a rut, but like most things, when you get used to it you can't even tell how bad it is anymore. We can get used to anything...pain, abuse, misery, stench, filth, boredom...they all become the norm after a time. For me it was mediocrity. I had never achieved my fullest potential and for awhile I fought it...then I accepted it. My life had become a grave...I did not know it when it happened, but in reality I was being buried alive.

So this summer, there was the usual graduations, weddings, graduations, birthdays, summer school, family gatherings, graduations, family gatherings, birthday, church functions, travel, graduations, church functions, family gatherings, weddings…yes, that seems about right. One of my many nieces was living with me, and one of my many nephews was back from college. There was every indication that my life would continue just the same as usual. There were just a few differences however: foreclosure, relocation, betrayal, a funeral, mango time, job loss, new friends, new beginnings, and renewed faith in God.

I cannot promise you that you will not face trials in your life, but I can promise you that when you put your trust in God, He will take you through. I can promise you too that your life will never be the same again once you make that step. You will be stronger, and more confident, and you will not ever walk in fear again...the scripture *For God hath not given us the spirit of fear; but of power, and of love, and of a sound mind,* 2 Tim. 1:7, will become very real, and you will be empowered to live – not just exist; to laugh- not just smile and nod, and to love without conditions. You will believe and know experientially that *no weapon that is formed against thee shall prosper; and every tongue that shall rise against thee in judgment thou shalt condemn. This is the heritage of the servants of the Lord, and their righteousness is of me, saith the Lord,* Is. 54:17.

The ensuing chapters is my attempt to

share with you how God pulled me out of that grave, and the lessons I learned as by His grace I weathered a storm which seemed unending. It was a storm made worse because there was no warning. There was no warning, then threat, then certainty. It was quick, brutal, and decisive. Each new dimension continued to take me by surprise. As I tried to cope with each problem, something else more amazingly painful would attack me. Eventually I realized that I was being ripped out of my comfort zone and I had little or no support to lean on…except God.

Part 1

The Phenomenon

CHAPTER 1

Traumatic Experiences

It would be a very special individual who had reached fifty and had not experienced trials. The most stressful experience that I have faced was when my mother who had Alzheimer's went missing. I was working at the College of Arts Science and Technology (now UTECH) in Kingston, Jamaica, when this happened. I remembered sitting at my desk when the 'phone rang and it was one of my nephews sharing the blood-chilling news. I immediately told my boss, the then president of the college, and he allowed me to leave work to help to search for my mother. At the end of the first day when I got home, (I was living in Kirkland Heights) I stood on my balcony which overlooked the city of

Kingston and just wept. The lights of the city which is always so spectacularly beautiful in the night became a labyrinth which caused despair. There was no beauty there, just a maze of light which in my mind was a trap for my mother. Which light would lead me there, was the question that tormented my mind. As I tossed and turned in sleepless misery, my only prayer was, "God, please help me find my mother, and please keep her from being hurt."

The next day I went back out to continue the search. By now more family members and friends had joined in the search. Fortunately for us, my mother had a famous son who has written and directed several plays; he was also an actor and a singer with the Jamaica National Dance Theater Singers, (NDTC), The Jamaica Folk Singers, The Little

Theatre Movement, (LTM), Pantomimes as well as starred in several locally produced documentaries and movies. The point is that once his friends and associates knew what had happened, it was well publicized in the media, and she was found soon after that, because of the many people who were now on the lookout for her.

Separation has always been a problem for me. I have problems even splitting up when I go shopping with a friend. Death is the ultimate separation because it is so final. When someone goes missing though, it can be worse than the separation of death because of the lack of closure. In my search I encountered an old woman who seemed to be wandering the streets as my mother would have been. I remember I had a banana in my hand, and I gave it to this old lady, and prayed that someone would show kindness to my mother even as I had shown kindness to this woman. My attitude to the poor and destitute has changed ever since that day. My mother miraculously was not hungry or hurt when she was returned to us. Someone took care of her; an angel perhaps? The ending I think could have been different were it not for divine intervention.

Then there was another brother, a police officer, who was kidnapped and killed. It took me many years to watch any movie that had any violence especially with the use of guns. I would keep reliving in my mind the horror, the pain the fear, and the anguish he must have felt, knowing that he was going to be murdered. Yes, that was sheer agony which took place in the year 1979.

Before that however, while I was at

teachers' college doing my final examinations, I got the news that my father had died. I remember the vice-principal taking me home that day. In that year I lost my father, a sister-in-law, and a nephew. In every one of those situations, I knew grief, pain, despair and the pain of separation.

These experiences and many more which will not be detailed in this book should have prepared me somewhat for what I went through, but I cannot say they did. Is anyone ever really prepared for the pain of betrayal, or the anguish of separation? I wasn't. I was in time able to draw on the inner strength provided by a daily walk with God, but initially, actions and reactions, took me off guard and made the wounds deeper and the healing slower.

CHAPTER 2

Encounter with an Angel

Some years ago while living in Florida, I had occasion to visit a friend specifically to have her purchase some material for a project which I was involved in at the church I was attending. The church represented Jamaica in the St. Petersburg International Folk Fair Society, (SPIFFS), which has an annual presentation of the culture of the many nations represented therein. It included a parade in which all the countries would wear the attire of their national costumes. That year for the first time, we agreed to march in the parade. We therefore needed the material to make the costumes. Luckily, I had a friend who was making a trip to Jamaica who had agreed to purchase the material for the church.

We had been at the church working steadily on some items for the Folk Fair until it was quite late. By the time I got to my friend's house to drop off the money needed to make the purchase, it had started to rain. It was close to midnight. My friend was up packing as she was leaving on a very early flight in the morning. Since I had to be at work at 7:00 a.m. we agreed that although it was late, I should still stop by even though it was raining. Neither of us wanted to chance waiting until morning in case we ran late. By the time I got to the door the light rain had become a torrential downpour. I was invited in to wait for the rain to abate and I gladly accepted the offer. We talked for awhile over some tea as she continued to pack. The rain continued steadily for what seemed like a very long time. Eventually I decided to leave in the rain, since we both had to make an early start in the morning. I was instructed not to drive on 9th Street which tended to flood when it rained. I took the advice. As I approached 6th street from 37th Avenue South, I realized that water was coming into the car. I glanced anxiously at the time and realized that it was close to 2:00 a.m. Almost immediately my fears turned into alarm as the car shut off. There, in the wee hours of the morning, I found myself alone and very afraid. It was the pre cell phone era, and getting out of the car to make a 'phone call did not seem like an option. On which door would I knock? Staying in the car seemed like the only option although it was not a solution by any means. The road seemed dark and gloomy. Sinister shadows seemed to lurk around street corners and behind trees. It was eerie. It was scary. But how would I get home? How would I get the car started again? The only thing I knew about cars was how to drive them. I was clueless as to how to even begin to help myself. I could not help myself. I was very scared. I needed a miracle.

Had I ever been in an untenable situation before? Had I ever needed a miracle before? Had God ever interceded miraculously on my behalf before? Yes, yes and yes to all three questions. As my fear turned to panic I remember praying, "I need a miracle right now!" As I looked out to 6th Street I saw a man dressed in a heavy, yellow raincoat. He was completely decked out with a yellow rain hat and water boots. He had a lantern in his hand and was walking with his head down as if he was looking to see what damage was done to the road. It struck me as odd that anyone would be out there examining the road at that time of morning. Yes, there was some construction going on, but nothing to warrant an investigation. It wasn't as if it was some major bridge or road that was being built which was in danger of being washed away. Despite the unlikely chance that this was the reason for the sudden appearance of the man in the yellow raincoat, I opted for that to be the explanation for his presence on the road at 2:20 a.m.

I was a little uneasy initially, and my first thought wasn't to ask for help. I did not feel fear, but I chose to remain as quietly in the car as possible. I wanted to exercise caution just in case the man in the yellow raincoat was up to no good. I was trying not to draw attention to myself. That decision was taken out of my hands as he looked up and started walking towards me. He came over to the car and I can't remember what his first words were, but

I know it had a calming effect. The next thing he said very clearly was "Do not get out of the car. I am going to push."

I did not touch the gears. I did not turn on the car. He was to the left side of the car and he started to push. The car instantaneously roared to life. I was overjoyed. I looked back to thank him but I did not see him anywhere. It took me many years later to really put that incident into perspective. I now am confident that God miraculously rescued me from that predicament. I was rescued by an angel. *For he shall give his angels charge over you, to keep you in all your ways, they shall bear thee up in their hands, lest thou dash thy foot against a stone,* Psalm 91:11-12. Do you believe in angels? I do! They are everywhere.

Certainly I believed that it was more

than coincidence that this man was there at the time. But only when I was reading a book which recounted stories about angelic interventions, did it dawn on me that I too had had an encounter with an angel. From that time I have shared my story many times, just wanting to help others to know that God is able and willing to help us in our times of need.

I have had several other supernatural encounters; some evil, some good. They remind me that we are in a constant battle between good and evil. Each battle we face is but a minute fraction of the existing warfare between these powers. On one side we have Satan and his demons, while on the other, we have God and His angels. But know this; Satan is not equal and opposite to God. He is already defeated! Unlike other battles, finite man really can only guess at the outcome, but in this war, Jesus has already won the victory.

When you are a Christian, you have the opportunity to help push back the forces of evil by lending a helping hand to those whom the enemy has singled out to be his next target. When we ignore those who are under demonic attack, we have chosen to stand with the enemy and to make a miserable situation more unbearable. It is easy to say to someone that "God will take care of you". It is just as easy and more meaningful to lend a helping hand. That hand of help may take a variety of forms. You may not have money but you may have time. Sometimes you just need to lend a listening ear. If you are on the Lord's side, He will guide you in the way you can help someone in need through their time of hardship and pain. These expressions of love will give strength and comfort to the one who has become Satan's latest target.

Unfortunately, too often our actions aid and abet the enemy, because instead of being there for the person under attack, we often make their situation worse by criticizing, demanding a specific action or behavior in exchange for our support, or making uninformed judgments. Thank God that not everyone is like that. God has angels right here on earth. Everyone who extends that helping hand is God's angel, and when as in my case with the car there was no-one there; He will send an angel from the heavenly host to rescue you from harm and dangers.

CHAPTER 3

My Spiritual Journey

I have often wondered about my spiritual journey. But I have come to realize that God has a plan for me which necessitates these various experiences. You see, like my brethren in some denominations I agree that there is only one way to heaven. That way however is not a denomination; it is not a law; it is not a day; it is not whether we sing with instruments or without instruments; it is not whether we shout or we whisper our prayers; it is not whether we clap our hands or keep them planted at our side, it not whether we pray standing or kneeling. It is rather a life that is sold out to Christ. It is a life that puts God first and practices the principles that he taught as He walked among men. That way is Jesus!

Because Jesus is the Perfect Sacrifice for the sins of the world and because He is the propitiation for our sins, we too can have life eternally. We too will be resurrected; we too will know forgiveness. Accepting Christ as our Savior simply means that we recognize Him as the only One that God will accept as righteous enough to take our place. Our gratitude and love for His grace and mercy makes us want to learn more about Him and to follow His footsteps.

A true Christian is one who knows that He can find strength in the unfailing love of Jesus. A true Christian is one who rests in the promises of Jesus. A true Christian is one who understands that life with Christ may be stormy, but we can smile yes, even laugh at the storm. A true Christian obeys God's laws because of the love which Jesus has shown. A true Christian understands the principle of sowing and reaping. A true Christian finds joy in the Christian life; for a true Christian, the Christian life it is not bondage, but freedom.

Each of the times I have switched denominations it has been because I have embraced some new truth. I do not see these changes as a sign of weakness but a sign of growth. Many people can boast of being in the same denomination or the same church all their lives. I would like to boast that I made a positive contribution to the lives I touched in the churches which I have attended.

It was in the Anglican (Episcopalian) Church that I had my first encounter with Christ. I remained an Anglican for many years, until my soul longed for more. The day that I got confirmed, the then Bishop of Kingston, Jamaica, shared a story with the confirmed candidates. It was a story about the refrigerator. He said that many times a refrigerator has old and stale food, which needs to be discarded. The refrigerator needs to be cleaned periodically so that the good stuff will not be contaminated. I understood on that day that a Christian's heart must be kept pure. As he put it; your heart now belongs to Jesus and He wants it to be as pure as He is. To an eleven year old, that message was simple and clear.

I really tried to keep my heart pure and it took me five years to hear a message that helped me to understand about confession and acceptance of Christ as Savior. This was through a visit to First Missionary Church in Kingston, Jamaica. I did what the Pastor said… when I went home. I was an Anglican, all my friends and family were Anglicans…

how could I become a member of the Missionary Church? My friend who had invited me, was in my opinion the embodiment of Christianity. I really wanted what she had. (Friends are indeed the best means of evangelism.) Again I tried to live what that pastor preached, but those seeds planted at my friend's church had no water to provide growth. As I continued in the church of my birth, I simply returned to living the Christian life as I always had. It took me six more years to walk down the aisle and publicly surrender to Jesus.

I had a hunger and thirst for the things of God. I enjoy writing but even as a teenager I had never had a desire to write anything that was not spiritual. Every play, every short story, every poem or song that I had ever written was an attempt to share my love for

Christ with others. After the secret surrender, my next major spiritual change was when I actually joined an evangelical church and got baptized. Now I was actually in a church which addressed the issues of living the Christian life. I enjoyed that church and denomination and remained a part of that congregation until I relocated to the United States. Despite the challenges, I continued to serve God and worshipped in many denominations as the Spirit led. From then on I continued to trust God.

Like the summer of 2009; my Christian life was not an easy road, but I thank all the pastors who have helped me to continue to trust God. Through all the uncertainties, I realize that it was never about what the Word teaches, but what we teach about the Word. Jesus is the Word! *"And the Word was made flesh, and dwelt among us, and we beheld his glory, the glory as of the only begotten of the Father, full of grace and truth,"* 1John1:14. Everything we see in Jesus Christ is the Word of God. There is no contradiction between the life of Jesus and the Bible; hence the confusion is not the Word and what it teaches; the confusion is what individuals choose to teach about the Word. *But the Comforter, which is the Holy Ghost, whom the Father will send in my name, he shall teach you all things, and bring all things to your remembrance, whatsoever I have said unto you,* John 14:26. God already knew that I would need help, so He promised to send The Holy Spirit to help me make important decisions concerning my walk with Him.

It seems though that the common thread that runs through all churches is not the undisputed love of God for all mankind, but the unrelenting judgment that one gets from many Christians within the church.

Sometimes people judge others by how they dress, what they eat, the type of car they drive, whom they marry, how well their children are doing, the church they attend, and by their level of education. If you actually fall, or if you seem to have messed up, or if you seem to have failed, some people see it as their duty; their divine right to tell you what to do. If you do not feel that their suggestion is best for you, do not expect to receive their help.

This happens in the church as well as in the world. It would seem that it does not matter how dedicated, giving, caring, and faithful to the teachings of the church an individual may be; in the end, your worth is often judged by material gain.

I remember a pastor telling me that I should get a better car because the one I was driving was not a reflection of God's wealth. He spoke of looking forward to the day when his church yard will be filled with top-of the-line cars, because wealth draws wealth. There is some truth in that but Christians ought not to be following the world. We ought to be hearing from an infallible loving God, who makes no mistakes. As such we should be leaders and not followers. *And the Lord shall make thee the head, and not the tail; and thou shalt be above only, and thou shalt not be beneath; if that thou hearken unto the commandments of the Lord thy God, which I command thee this day, to observe and to do them.* Deuteronomy 28:13

People do tend to cause others pain. I am definitely not exempt from that shortcoming. I have done things which bother me to this day and I certainly hope to make amends. I would hate to be the reason for individuals to stumble. The Word of God speaks strongly to this issue. *Let us not therefore judge one another anymore: but judge this rather, that no man put a stumbling block or an occasion to fall in his brother's way.* Romans 14:13. God ought not be judged and discarded because some of us send mixed signals. As Christians we know better. There could be no excuse for someone like me to turn my back on the church when I have enjoyed the blessings of God in my life. So I had experienced betrayal before, even in the church; but it still did not prepare me for the summer of 2009.

CHAPTER 4

Who is to be Blamed?

Whose fault was it anyway? Why even get angry or upset? I was where I was because of ignorance in part, and because of the way I chose to spend the blessings which God had given me. The willingness to take responsibility for the things which happen to us is a huge part of being able to get up and start again.

Sometimes we are victims, and sometimes we are disadvantaged. Usually in these situations one party is incapable of fighting back. This is not what is being addressed here. I was not prepared to buy a house. I had no background information and had a mortgage that was way too high for the thirteen years that I had been a homeowner. It was then that I really understood the nature of the battle I was fighting.

Once I saw what was happening I knew that a decision had to be made. The decision was a tough one. You imagine the eyes of embarrassment; the whispered words of condescension; the condemnation and the judgment. The world will always want you to do what seems to look good. The world is not of God though, and so in making the decision I recognized those who were friends and those who were foes; those who were materialistic and those who were spiritual. The decision had to be made and I made it. How amazing it was that instead of sinking into an abyss of despair, I was lifted out of my uncertainty and given a new sense of determination and hope and peace!

My peace I give unto you: not as the world give, give I

unto you. Let not your heart be troubled, neither let it be afraid. John 14:27.

The peace I felt when I decided to let the house go, took me by surprise. I had expected to be miserable...I had used all my savings and pension to invest in a home that I would now be losing. I could not even point to my children to say that this was where my money had been spent. I couldn't because I have no children. It seemed that my life was futile. I felt like I was worse than a piece of driftwood washed up on the sand. I felt as if I were something that someone would step on, or walk by, and not even notice. Yet when I made the decision I felt good. It had to be supernatural! A few well-meaning individuals made some suggestions as to how I could save the house, but each time I attempted to embrace those Ideas I became so depressed and burdened that I knew that those suggestions were not for me. I knew that they were the counterfeit.

Almost as if to ensure that I would be resolute, about giving up the house, the greatest temptation presented itself. This involved an individual who works as a loan modification employer in a bank. In this job he was able to learn all the tricks of the trade and perhaps would have been able to help me to save the house if anyone could. That night after he spoke to me, I had no peace. I just could not sleep. I was so tormented in my spirit that I became literally nauseous. By morning I called and told him that I would not accept his offer to work out a plan. I was instantly at peace again. So now what....I had a supernatural peace, but the world that can only see things in measurable gain, sees a not so young woman who has nothing. They see failure.

Often when individuals encounter people who have apparently failed, they feel they have the right to pass judgment. You have nothing so, you have no feeling...you are no longer alive...you can't feel. People who know nothing about you feel that they have a right to offer advice, demean you, and ridicule you. Since you have no worth, they can call you crazy, stupid and hasty. So yes, I suffered all of that and I held on. What I did not realize was that those experiences were the least of my problems.

In losing my house I made a startling discovery. I did not own my house. I was just renting. I was called a homeowner, but I was renting from the bank, and renting from the bank I discovered, was infinitely worse than renting from a private homeowner. That information more than anything else is what prepared me for the next phase of my life.

Being called a homeowner is a misnomer. Anyone who has recently lost their home, or is about to lose it, or is struggling to keep up with the current payments suddenly comes face to face with that truth. Many handle it philosophically...others - not so much. It was at that precise moment that the idea of sharing my experience with the world came to me. In writing this book I hope to say there is life after loss; any loss, losing a home not excluded. I would like to save them the anguish that I experienced and give them some stepping stones to help them make it.

Three groups of people stand to benefit: the ones who have lost their homes and feel hopeless, the ones who are in the whirlpool of debts and are trying to hold on to their homes, and finally those who haven't bought a home as yet. For those who are not in any of these categories; perhaps you can pass the intelligence on to someone else.

It was my fault. I should have done my homework. I didn't. I want to help others to understand the need to make sure that they know the facts. I hope that when someone else decides to rent from the bank that person understands what the best course of action to take.

CHAPTER 5

The Gathering Storm

I bought the house not for its aesthetic value, but for its size. Since I was already living in the house, it made it even more reasonable to buy that house. The owner was planning to sell and I decided to hold on to it because it was perfectly suited for my tutoring business. It had two front entrances and enough space to conduct the business on one side without encroaching on my personal living space at all. I had had that business for three years before the owner decided to sell. I did not come out the winner even in that deal. But the deed was done, I was a homeowner.

When President Obama started his presidential campaign for the 2008 elections and explained sub-prime mortgages and all the attendant drama, I immediately realized that I was one of those people who really should not have been given a mortgage. My problems began very soon after I signed that piece of paper and they continued to escalate until I lost the house.

The problems were compounded because using the house as a business meant that I had to keep the light and the water on which sometimes meant that the mortgage would be late or not paid because I did not get paid on time by my clients. Common sense should have told me to sell and move on; but if it did, I either did not hear or was not listening. The only voice I heard was the one which kept telling me to save the house.

I was working two jobs and managed for nine years to hold on to both of them. In 2007 I gave up my night job but was invited back soon after. I used much of my savings to remodel the house and I also refinanced it. In a very short space of time I had spent over $35,000.00 on this house. This included a brand new kitchen built by my brother-in-law - one of the best in the business - new carpet for the bedrooms, tiles for the living room and the family room, plus new furniture throughout the house. Would anyone spend that much money on something that does not belong to them? I did, because I was a homeowner... or so I thought.

In June 2008, I resigned again from my night job. This time it was also because I just couldn't handle two jobs and study at the same time. But 2008, was the year the economy went south and I felt the ripple effects of that with no cushion on which to fall.

My mortgage was just under $2,000.00 monthly. Initially the problem was just the income loss from the night job, and with stipends and frugal living I could perhaps have survived without it. Once I started losing students, I knew trouble was on the horizon and I could see the storm clouds gathering. I fell behind and tried to keep up. I was placed on a forbearance plan which was difficult to pay because it pushed the mortgage payment even higher. In the end I lost the house because I made the payment late on a day that I had agreed to make it. I fell asleep and forgot to call it in. When offered the Obama loan modification plan, I thought I had been approved and was waiting for the letter, but it never came, what came in the mail was the final judgment against me... my house was officially in foreclosure. I had received the initial foreclosure letter sometime while waiting for the loan modification. They told me not to worry, the process would continue but I would soon hear from them.

The letter of foreclosure was therefore a great shock to me and turned my life upside down. There was so much hanging on that modification coming through! When I realized that it was not going to happen, and that losing my house was imminent, my sense of despair and hopelessness was indescribable. It suddenly occurred to me that after all these years of working; I had nothing to show for it.

I am not a person who likes to hide things. My belief is that people will know about what you are hiding anyway. I made it clear to family and friends that I lost my home.

Many close friends and family by way of

encouragement reminded me of my accomplishments. Some friends and family members reminded me how important I was to them and how many people I had helped. Some prayed with me and called me often just to make sure I was okay. There are those who alluded to my strength "You are really so strong, you will make it." they said. Some of my friends took the time to visit with me, and took me out to lunch and dinner, gave me CD's with songs of encouragement. Those were dark days, but always there was the hope that it would get better.

All this time I was very conscious of the presence of God in my life. When the devil knocks us down and we seem to be out for the count, God will send as many angels as is needed to pull us through. For everyone who turned their back on me, there were three times as many friends or family to encourage and support me. All this happened in the summer of 2009.

CHAPTER 6

Rain and Sunshine

Teachers look forward to summer. It is a time to relax and replenish, body, mind and spirit. Most teachers are drained in many ways by the end of the school year. I was no different. To present the incidents in real time, I will begin with a trip to Michigan for a nephew's graduation. At that graduation, the fit of my clothes told me that I had a weight problem. I felt very uncomfortable in my clothes. As I looked at myself in the full length mirror, I decided that when I got back home to St. Petersburg, Florida I would start walking as a form of exercise. I had done this before with excellent results. I had stopped walking though, when my knee started hurting so badly that I was limping from the pain. I remember my then pastor having to do surgery on his knee and wondered if that was to be my fate also.

My sister who had watched me limping and struggling to climb stairs said to me "Pauline you will walk again without the pain." That was said with so much confidence that I just had to believe her. She said it because the same thing had happened to her when she had been walking and also had had to stop walking. But now she walks just fine. So I did start walking again "without the pain"…but soon I stopped. The weight of course returned with enthusiastic vengeance. Graduation in Michigan in May 2009 was my wake up call.

I went back home and I started a walking regimen again. In a very short time the results were evident. I had living with me at the time a niece who was a health nut or nugget depending on what she is saying to you and what your frame of mind is. She was very encouraging to me. She always celebrated with me every ounce that I lost and suggested ways to improve. My goal had been to lose 75 pounds, so that I would be 145 lbs. I still had 35 lbs to lose. I had lost more than forty pounds in a thirteen month period. This was not monumental, but considering I was not on a special diet plan I was happy with the results.

I would walk five miles on weekdays and try to do at least seven miles on weekends and during the holidays. I drank a lot of water; ate lots of fresh fruits and vegetables and I had cut back on fats, sugar and salt and I tried to stay away from anything made with flour. With all of these foods removed eating became a challenge, but I focused on what I could eat rather than what I couldn't and I was amazed just how many good meals I was able to make during that time.

Although not a vegetarian, I eat meat sparingly. I stay away from fast foods as much as possible, and my restaurants of choice would be Thai restaurants and sometimes Chinese, because they do serve lots of vegetable dishes. I lost four dress sizes in that thirteen month period.

The next major event was a wedding in Jamaica. I elected not to go. I was holding on to my cash because I was not sure what kind of funds would be required when the modification came through. I chose not to go because of the time factor. I had already taken time off for the graduation in Michigan; I did not want to take more time off from the students I tutor, especially just before their big exams. I was also working on my Masters in Education Leadership. I did not want to go off to Jamaica and have to worry about funds and assignments when I should be relaxing and enjoying a wedding.

The summer was taking shape. I was broke though. I had not had a good year financially and was behind in my mortgage. I was waiting to hear about the loan modification but in the mean time I was trying to have a good summer. The next major event was the graduation held for the students whom I tutored. As I listened to the glowing accolades I felt encouraged that my labor had not gone unrecognized. I had two kindergarten graduates, two fifth grade graduates and one eighth grade graduate.

Coming to America means you leave many friends and family behind. Here in St.

Petersburg I had a childhood friend whose mom passed while I was visiting in Fort Lauderdale. One of my nephews and I, accompanied a niece, (the health nut living with me), to Fort Lauderdale so that she could pick up some of the things she had left behind when she had moved to St. Petersburg. It was while there that I received the call from my childhood friend that her mother had died. I made the decision to go to Jamaica for the funeral. While in Fort Lauderdale we stayed with another nephew and his wife. He was brother of the nephew traveling with us and yes my niece's cousin. While there we embarked on some pretty interesting adventures which surrounded the acquisition of mangoes and coconuts. You see, Jamaicans - most of us that is, absolutely love mangoes and there is such a wide variety that it would be almost impossible for me to name them all.

Everyone has a favorite, but most mango lovers will eat whatever kind they can get, especially when living in the United States.

Before we left St. Petersburg, we told family and friends that we would be embarking on a "mango run", in Fort Lauderdale. This meant that we would be visiting the homes of anyone we knew who had mangoes. In fact we sent the word out that we would be coming so that they would have the mangoes ready for us. We were so excited about the prospect of getting these mangoes that on the first trip we were (or maybe more accurately), I was singing a famous Jamaican folk song called Mango Time. I will share the lyrics with you, just in case you want to sing along.

Mango Time

Mi nuh drink coffee tea mango time

Care how nice it may be mango time

In the heat of the mango crop

When di fruit dem a ripe an drop

Wash your pot turn dem down mango time

De turpentine large an fine, mango time

Robin mango so sweet, mango time

Number eleven an hairy skin

Pack di bankra an ram dem in

For di bankra mus' full, mango time

Mek wi go a mango walk, mango time

For is only di talk mango time

Mek wi jump pon di big jackass

Ride im dung an no tap a pass

Mek di best a di crop, mango time[1]

You are right…it is written in Jamaican
dialect.

When we got to Fort Lauderdale we had such great success that we named it *Mango Run 2009*. I must make a clarification here, my nephew is American born and my niece migrated here when she was only nine.

They are very versed in the dialect and the culture however and so the appreciation. My nephew was probably with us more for the thrill of the acquisition of the fruit than eating the fruit itself. We brought back many mangoes that time. Because of the funeral, I was back there with my niece and nephew again. They remained in Fort Lauderdale until I returned. As soon as I returned, we embarked on *Mango Run 2009 Part 2*. It was wonderful! The last thing on my mind was foreclosure. But yes, that unfortunately is exactly what was waiting for me when I got back home to St. Petersburg, Florida.

I received the letter telling me that the house had a final judgment on it and after getting a "niece" to explain what that meant, I finally allowed myself to fall apart and begin the painful process of sharing the information with friends and family.

So I fall apart, but I am thinking of ways to save my home. The mortgage company tells me I need $23,000.00 to save the house. As I said before I had spent most of my savings in fixing up the house. There was other monies being spent on the house for another reason and that contributed to my distress. It was not a good time for me at all. I called a few people to get advice and most of the suggestions were the same. The bottom line was that there did not seem to be a way out. When you are self employed it seems like getting loans is the hardest thing to achieve.

When I made the decision to let the house go, it was difficult, but as difficult as it was everything that followed that decision was infinitely worse. I called my sister in Jamaica but she couldn't talk to me, she had a dental appointment…then I called my niece her daughter and she really gave me sobriety. She was so positive and so calming, that I actually felt that yes, I can do this. I spoke to my sister in Jamaica the next day. She also encouraged me and told me that whatever decision I made she would support me as best as she could.

The Friday of that week I was getting an oil change and I called my sister again and told her my decision. She confirmed that this is what she had felt through her prayers that I should do, but wanted to hear what my decision would be. I knew my sister would have helped me as much as she could if I had decided to try to keep the house. However, keeping the house did not seem like a good idea. I would not have the benefit of a loan modification and to get the money to save the house would have meant borrowing money. I did not see any way in which I could have made it. When that young man from the bank, (the loan modification expert), had made his recommendation, yes it did seem great, but I somehow knew it was not for me. I had to let my house go. This decision was not well-accepted by some, but there were good reasons not to accept certain other suggestions. I will not detail that aspect of the drama except to say that I was certain that the decision to let the house go was the right one.

When I had finished getting the oil change, I just about completed my conversation with my sister in Jamaica and I was heading downtown to pay my water bill.

On my way there I saw a house which was not unattractive, but seemed a little small. I passed the house and then an inner voice said "come back around and take the number down". The voice was so insistent that I obeyed it. I eventually rented the house.

[1] Mango Time, (2004) , Jamaican Culture.

http://www.jamaicans.com/culture/folk/mangot.shtml

CHAPTER 7

Tsunami

Many people may have wondered why I did not take the opportunity to remain in the house for the five months which it usually takes for a foreclosure to become final. I did not have that luxury. A portion of my house was being remodeled to be used as a church. There was ample space for the purpose, and I agreed to it because I was happy to give this new work a start. What I did not realize when I agreed to have my house used for a church, was how extensive the remodeling would be, and how long it would have taken.

The work had started from the summer of 2008 and one year later the work was not completed. That had already caused some tension because as I stated, I had not expected that it would have taken so long.

My concern about this had already caused a decision to be made the very week of the final judgment of the foreclosure. On the evening when we should meet to discuss what would be done, I was too overwhelmed with despair to even sit in the meeting. That Wednesday morning I had sought to get some advice from someone I thought was in real estate, but I found out that she wasn't. Everyone in America had a foreclosure story to share however, so she shared her near miss and her daughter's hit and prayed with me and suggested I let the house go. That night, I asked my "niece", a lawyer, to explain what the letter meant and she told me that I was in the process of losing the house. She spoke of doing a quick sale and allowing a certain family member to buy the house so that I would be able to live there. I did not want to go that route however, and hence decided not to pursue the suggestion. For reasons I will not share, I knew that the suggestion though well meant was not a tenable one.

A meeting was convened to discuss the impasse regarding the length of time being taken to complete the renovations on the house to accommodate the church. However my current emotional state made the thought of sitting in on that meeting quite unbearable. I told them to go ahead without me, I had already told some of them about the foreclosure but the meeting was about finding another venue for the church. I did not see how I could have remained in the house for another five months. The house was still not completed and my tutoring service was about to restart in three weeks. I needed to have a permanent place to start the school year.

After declining to be a part of the meeting I went to the park and sat in my car and spoke to my niece in Jamaica, who gave me a lot of encouragement. I did not return home until my family had left. I had three papers to write for the current class I was taking, and I had many arrangements to make. I felt that I was going to lose my mind because of all the pressure I was feeling. Yet all the time there was a sense of inner peace and calm.

So much had happened in the three weeks before the tutoring service restarted, that any attempt to put the events in words would make it seem incredible. I single handedly packed up everything in my house and moved. I made several small trips in my car; I rented the house and cleaned it out. My nephew accompanied me on a couple of those trips. I had a friend to help me with some other not so large items, and then I rented a truck for the larger items. I switched all my utilities and tried to make sure that everything would be up and running so that I could continue my studies without interruption. I continued to walk and to pray. I moved hastily because I had two students in particular who were to graduate that year and I didn't want them to have to interrupt their studies.

This may seem disingenuous to some but it is nonetheless the truth. These two students had been with me since they were babies. They were now about to enter the eighth grade. I was not sure that when it was time to move I would have found the right place and be able to move. Besides the complication with the construction on my home would most likely get worse. Tutoring there would be almost impossible - that is how it seemed to me anyway. So I moved and lost the funds I could have possibly saved by staying in the house rent free for another five months.

It was now time for our first meeting of the school year. This was held ten days before school would reopen. It was then that I discovered that five of the nine students whom I tutored would not be returning.

Two of the five students were the ones who precipitated the early move. I was really surprised by the turn of events. I had already told them of the location of the school and they had seen the place. I took that to mean that they were okay with the choice. But how wrong I was! As I sat there in disbelief at the supreme irony of the situation, I could only call out to God in my spirit. I asked Him to help me to make the right decisions. In the natural I tried to reason with them, but they had come with a made up mind; find another place or they would not return.

I can't even attempt to describe my mortification, my embarrassment and my shame. I felt like a dog that was cold and hungry and saw what appeared to be a light in the distance. With every vestige of strength he struggles towards the light, certain that it would be alright. The light meant hope, warmth, and a meal, but as he gets to the light, it is put out and he is alone again. I was that dog, and these parents were my hope. I expected them to hang with me ...I expected it because our relationship was more than just business, but I was wrong. I had lost my house, I was a failure, I lived in the wrong neighborhood; I was to be discarded like yesterday's porridge. Because of the nature of the relationship with these parents, I had just naturally assumed that they would hang in there with me. I learned a lot about human nature in that moment. I also realized that my biggest failure was to see people as my hope and not God. God is a jealous God. All glory belongs to Him. I was wrong to have placed my hope in these parents and that was made very clear.

"Did they have a right to remove their children? They certainly did, but I was not prepared for it to happen, nor was I prepared for the seemingly callous way in which it was done. I was the person who was at fault though. My actions were based on false assumptions about them, when the only certainty was in the whispered words of a God whose directions oftentimes seem contrary to everything that makes sense. I erroneously assumed that if God was telling me to move on, that He was telling them that it would be alright to stay with me.

They wanted me to find another place to continue the tutoring service. They were not being mean, I suppose. They just felt that my choice of venue was not upscale enough for their children. None of my suggestions was good enough; therefore the suggestion was that they would keep their children home until I found something suitable. They left on that note.

Edgar Allan Poe says, "Believe only half of what you see and nothing of what you hear".[1] The accolades given at the graduation inspired confidence that the parents were indeed satisfied with what they were getting from me as a tutor, but how quickly that changed! My worth was not measured, (it seems to me) by my teaching abilities, but by the neighborhood in which I now resided.

In a moment of weakness I had agreed to give it a try - to find another place that is - but just as the last couple was about to leave, a voice from within asked, "What are you doing?" It would have been a disaster! Renting two places would require even more funds than when I struggled with the one mortgage.

Before the last two walked out the door I told them that I would not be looking for a place but that we would start as usual, even if it were four students. At that time I wasn't even sure of four, because when the parents of those five stated their decision to move on; other parents had begun to feed off their negativity. By the end of the meeting I was sure of only one student out of the nine. It was a very horrific experience. But I had my God and a few friends to lean on. I did not tell any family member of this latest setback. If they knew it was not through me. I continued my walking regimen and I continued to lose weight. I continued to pray and I continued to trust God. I continued to listen to my CDs. I continued to receive encouragement from some family and friends here and abroad. I continued to trust God and to pray and to walk, and to lose weight. I went to a different church and tried to heal. The process was slow…almost imperceptible.

[1]goodreadsInc, 2014. Edgar Allan Poe, Quotes. http://www.goodreads.com/quotes/252780-believe-only-half-of-what-you-see-and-nothing-that

CHAPTER 8

God is Good

One day I heard laughter and realized it was mine. But this was a long time after that fateful parents meeting, when knives were turned in an already painful wound. It would be easy to say that when I made the decision to open "school" as usual, that I had no concerns…easy but untrue. I had no idea what would happen, but I was sure of one thing… just as God wanted me to let my house go and move to this new location for the tutoring; it was also God who had encouraged me not to look elsewhere for yet another place to do tutoring, but to continue where I was located as planned.

It was my job now to inform those who had not come to the meeting and everyone who had left before I had made the decision to open as usual that tutoring would start as scheduled. I wasn't sure what to expect when I made the call. It turned out that the ones who wanted changes *did* take their children out. The others all decided to return and that brought the number up to five. This happened because a parent who had had only one student attending in the previous year now decided to send a second child. Then two of the parents who were present at the meeting but had shown uncertainty, called and said their children would be starting school with me... now I was up to seven.

On the Sunday before the Tuesday when school would reopen, I spoke to another parent, who said that I came highly recommended. After a few questions and the initial visit he sent his two boys to me. I now had exactly the number of students enrolled that I had expected to have before the meeting convened. Miraculously l went from 1 to nine. We have to know the voice of God and more importantly, we have to obey it. By January my enrollment went up to ten.

I went to a different church, just to be alone and to heal. I did not want the added stress of having to accept positions in church as has always been the case. The church I attended was a very significant part of my healing. I made a new friend, and became reacquainted with another. The music from the choir really blessed and encouraged me. The church did for me what churches should do help struggling individuals to find hope and peace in the midst of their storm. It is ironical that this church which was having more than its fair share of problems was where I found peace.

It was one of the best years of the school. We had a wonderful graduation. I also completed my Masters program and had kept off the weight I had lost. So what did I learn from my experience?

Part 2

The Lessons Learned

CHAPTER 9

Communication

Every living creature is able to communicate among themselves. It may be very simple or it may be very complex. Humans, the most intelligent of all the species also communicate among themselves. Yet it would seem that humans have an amazing propensity to miscommunication than any other species on the planet. The results of miscommunication are often devastating. *For if the trumpet gives an uncertain sound, who shall prepare himself to the battle?* 1Corinthians 14:8.

There are many ways in which humans fail to communicate effectively. But verbal communication oftentimes gets us in a lot of trouble. Many times we just did not explain clearly enough what we intended to convey. Other times miscommunication occurs because we are distracted. This distraction may be attributed to anything which is capable of blocking the individual from clearly receiving the information transmitted. For example if an individual is seen as a liar, it will not matter in many instances if he is telling the truth, preconceived knowledge will often prevent individuals from "hearing" his version. The same holds true for a person known for his integrity. Such a person may be a pathological liar but individuals will listen to that person against another individual who may be giving the correct version of an incident. Bias then is a huge distraction and so communication often gets skewed. In my time of trouble it seems there were many miscommunications. Isn't it wonderful to know then, that God our heavenly Father is omnipresent and omniscient? *For whenever our heart condemns us, God is greater than our heart, and he knows everything.*1 John 3:20. Here is what I learned.

- ❖ Effective communication produces clarity and reduces misunderstanding
- ❖ Both receiver and transmitter should be dedicated to understanding the essence of the communication.
- ❖ It is okay to ask for clarification. That is much better than saying "I thought you said…" or "I thought you meant…"
- ❖ Patience is an invaluable virtue in the achievement of effective communication.

❖ Poor communication will almost always, destroy, or frustrate friendships, alienate family members, and cause confusion which produces unnecessary rifts.

❖ Always be willing to assume that there was a misunderstanding when communication produces conflict.

❖ When there is conflict and strife, make haste to find a resolution. Never be satisfied when even one person is alienated. Jesus wouldn't.

How think ye? if a man have an hundred sheep, and one of them be gone astray, doth he not leave the ninety and nine, and goes into the mountains, and seeks that which is gone astray" Matthew 18:12

CHAPTER 10

Buying a House

I did not do my homework. I did not study. I was therefore unprepared. I failed the test. Imagine that! I, a teacher for many years did not do my homework. I learned a few things however.

- ❖ Live frugally and save until you can come up with a good down payment. The money you will save in interest and tax will be well worth the wait.

- ❖ It is a good idea to avoid refinancing and remodeling...remember you are only renting from the bank and if you lose your house you will have give away a fortune.

- ❖ If you have extra money...pay it to the principal, but in this frazzled economy…I would hold on to my extra cash…just in case.

❖ When you have a mortgage you are just renting from the bank. The title of homeowner gives a feeling of good will and rightly so. However, if I had not bought the house and lived in the house to which I moved in the ten years I lived there, I could have saved $100,000 dollars. But let's say my income fluctuated, or I did not save consciously I am willing to say I would have had enough to buy one of the many foreclosed homes. This is why friends, "the rich gets richer". That American dream, that says "own a home" is not as clear-cut as it seems, in fact for many of us especially middle class single income home owners, this is often a nightmare.

- Renting from the bank means taking care of someone's bills and paying their interests and their taxes, for the misnomer of being called a homeowner.

- Owning a home is a good thing. I would be a hypocrite to say that it is anything less. When planning to own a home, do it the right way. Make sure you do the research and think about what will happen if you lose some or all of your income for any reason; sickness, job loss, and divorce are some reasons which come to mind.

- When you buy a home, the end should be in sight. That way you can really enjoy it.

- I intend to learn by my mistakes.. *Come now, you who say, "Today or tomorrow we will go into such and such a town and spend a year there and trade and make a profit"— yet you do not know what tomorrow will bring. What is your life? For you are a mist that appears for a little time and then vanishes. Instead you ought to say, "If the Lord wills, we will live and do this or that."* James 4: 13-15. If the Lord wills I will own another house.

CHAPTER 11

Family

I grew up in a very close family. When I was teaching at Alpha Academy in Jamaica and I received news that my brother was killed, I was very distraught. I was in tears and as I was getting ready to go home, I remember one of the teachers saying, "I guess you were close". It struck me as odd at the time because I did not understand the concept of "not being close to family members".

As the situation unfolded it was evident that for whatever reason, there were individuals in my family who were going to make it really hard to move forward. Like everything else you have to decide…do I want to fight for my family or not. Many individuals even in my family are callous enough to just let family and friends go...losing family and friends is of no consequence to them. But in the changing fortunes of time we never know how the wind will blow. Today we may feel strong enough to conquer the universe, so we tread hard. We have no feelings for family members with hands outstretched for help, or comfort. They are an embarrassment...they are an irritant...we do not need them.

Keeping in touch with family is not about needs however...you may really not need them...in fact they may indeed be a bother, an embarrassment, a pest...yet God gave us our family. If God will never leave us nor forsake us, *Be strong and of a good courage, fear not, nor be afraid of them: for the LORD thy God, he it is that doth go with thee; he will not fail thee, nor forsake thee*, Deuteronomy 31:6, wretched as we are, who are we to forsake our family and trample over them especially in their time of need?

It takes much more energy anyway, to stay angry than to forgive and forget. Many may think you are weak, but actually it takes a lot of strength to reach out to persons who have hurt you when you know that you really did nothing to deserve the treatment received.

❖ We all need our family members; they are God's gift to us. If we shed some of them, we inevitably weaken ourselves, since we are all links of the same chain. As we weaken our family we weaken our society and that circle of weakness only becomes wider and wider.

❖ Forgiving and moving forward is much better than staying angry and standing still. Most times everyone is waiting on you to make the first move. If you dare to do so; you will find, (in time), that it was the right thing to do.

❖ Ignore that little voice that tells you to hold on to your pride; your pride is not worth a can of beans when you are alone and long to share treasured memories with your loved ones in your family.

❖ Whole heartedly I cling to the statement *Behold, how good and how pleasant it is for brethren to dwell together in unity,* Psalm 133:1 and regardless how difficult it may become, I strive for that unity or harmony with members of my family.

CHAPTER 12

Friends

I like having friends. When I was a child, I learned this jingle from my elementary school teacher:

Have many a friend; treat them well,

But never to them have your secrets tell

For when your friends become your foes,

Out over the world you secret goes.

"When your friends become your foes?" Are you kidding me? Who is waiting until a friendship ends, to share "nice juicy gossip?" Everyone talks about others…even best friends. I like having friends nonetheless, and I will prefer to take the risk of losing a friend than not to have friends at all. So what have I learned from this experience about friends…

❖ They are able to hurt and betray more than anyone else

❖ Not all friends will stand by you in times of need.

❖ If a friend does not stand by you in times of need; sometimes they just can't. Not everyone is strong.

❖ A friend should not be judged because of one incident…check the history.

❖ You can be a friend to someone who is not necessarily a friend to you.

❖ True friends remain your friends even if you haven't talked to them for years. They are happy to hear from you, they weep with you; they try to find ways to make you smile and they hold on with you until they are sure that you are able to stand on your own. *A friend loveth at*

all times, and a brother is born for adversity.
Proverbs 17:17

❖ True friends are like gems...rare and precious. It is worth it to cherish those relationships as you would a treasure.

❖ Jesus is the best Friend...He is never too busy to listen and to answer...His wisdom surpasses all others...and he gives us calm in the storm...that is a friendship which never fails. *Greater love hath no one than this, that a man lay down his life for his friends.* John 15:13

CHAPTER 13

Helping Others

It is a good thing to help others. *Bear you one another's burdens, and so fulfill the law of Christ.* Galatians 6:2. It is easy to think of helping only in the financial arena. But bearing one another's burden makes it clearer. An individual's burden, (or need), may be any of the following: financial, spiritual, companionship, personal care, home care transportation, food, quality time, encouragement or many other needs which we encounter at various stages in our lives. As Christians we are called to give help. Unfortunately for most people, help when given often becomes a burden to the one who receives.

A person may decide to help you and you find yourself locked into a relationship which often leaves you more oppressed than before. For many, help when given has a price. You are subtly reminded of the help given, and as a result of that help a certain behavior is expected. Unless there was a business arrangement, help given should have no hidden demands. Since I am certain that every person who will read this book has either helped someone in the past, or has needed and received help, let me share what I have learned.

❖ Expect a blessing when you help others. *He that hath a bountiful eye shall be blessed...*Proverbs 22:9

❖ It is best to give help with no strings attached.

❖ When you give help to someone, do not expect that the blessing which is promised to those who help others will necessarily come from the individual you have helped; most likely it will not.

❖ When your heart tells you to help someone; listen to that voice. The negative thoughts which tend to dissuade you are often from the enemy and not from God.

❖ If you decide to help someone leave that individual with dignity. Do not lecture and berate the individual as to your beliefs regarding the reasons why that person is in need of help or has fallen into hard times. That lecture may be necessary, but it may not be your job. Your job may be just to help because you are able to do so.

- ❖ The Bible tells that we *reap what we sow,* Galatians 6:7: in other words our reward will be in kind. If we sow love we will receive love. If we sow friendship we will be blessed with good friends, and if we help someone in need of financial help we will be blessed in our bank account.

- ❖ Be sincere in your help. A grudging spirit will not be blessed.

- ❖ Remember, in helping others, God is our reward!

Then shall the King say unto them on his right hand, Come, ye blessed of my Father, inherit the kingdom prepared for you from the foundation of the world:

For I was an hungred, and ye gave me meat: I was thirsty, and ye gave me drink: I was a stranger, and ye took me in:

Naked, and ye clothed me: I was sick, and ye visited me: I was in prison, and ye came unto me. Matthew 25:34-36

CHAPTER 14

Health and Fitness

I remember when I shared my "Summer of Distress" with a friend, she responded by saying "It is such a blessing that you were on an exercise regimen. It kept you from becoming depressed." Then she went on to share her knowledge of the relationship between exercise and feeling good. I checked a few web-sites and I choose to share this comment.

Exercise decreases the stress hormones such as cortical and increases endorphins. Endorphins are the body's natural feel good chemicals, and when they are released through exercise, your mood is boosted naturally. As well as endorphins, exercise also releases adrenaline, serotonin, and dopamine. These chemicals work together to make you feel good[1].

Isn't God awesome? Now you may be wondering how I jumped from endorphins to a comment about God; but for the Christian there are no coincidences. I have had summers when I was unhappy and depressed even when I had my home and things were going well. I was miserable because it seemed like I was getting nowhere; but the summer when I lost my house…I was exercising and losing weight and I was studying and getting excellent grades. All of these experiences combined to help me to get through that period which could have driven me insane.

My friend was right. Thank God it didn't happen at any other time…Thank God I was mentally, physically, emotionally, and most importantly spiritually prepared to handle the nightmare. To God is the glory! So what did

I learn about exercise?

- ❖ It helps your body to provide its own natural pain medicine.

- ❖ You feel good because your body is producing hormones to make you feel good and because you are losing weight, you want to continue to exercise; which makes you feel even better...a good catch 22!

- ❖ It is not easy to get started, but start slowly and set attainable goals

- ❖ Just never stop exercising...even when you have binged on your favorite junk food...that box of doughnut, or chocolate, or ice cream...whatever it is. Just continue to exercise.

❖ If you are thinking about starting an exercise regimen…start now.

❖ Exercise is for everyone…young and old, overweight or healthy… it is just a good thing to do.

❖ Sometimes you get to a plateau. My nephew shared with me that it took him a long time to get past his plateau, but he persevered.

❖ Persevere when it seems as if you will not lose another pound. Never give up instead change your exercise routine. Add more miles or more weight but never give up. Change your diet plan; sometimes you actually need to eat more. Persevere until you reach your goal

❖ Walking to the store or to a park is a good way to increase daily exercise. Instead of looking for the parking space nearest to the building I am about to enter I now park a good distance away and give myself that extra few yards to walk. Every little counts.

❖ I increased my exercise by adding weights, climbing stairs, or doing a dance exercise regimen alone or better still with friends.

❖ I have always exercised alone and this can be very important because you are not dependent on others. However, working in a group can be a good addition to your weight loss program.

This provides motivation. At one time I agreed with some other individuals who walked at the park around the same time each morning to set individual weight loss goal. It helped to be accountable to others.

[1] Natural Therapy Pages –Australia's #1 natural health site.

(http://www.naturaltherapypages.com.au/article/Exercise_Endorphins)

CHAPTER 15

People

People are people...we are as different and as similar as the sand on the seashore or as the stars in the sky. I learned or perhaps solidified my thoughts about people because of my experience, and here is what I will share.

❖ People do not make or break us...we do that to ourselves

❖ People have the same needs; happiness, love, companionship, friendship, peace, joy, and comfort. When deprived of these basic needs, people become less like people and more like animals. Now they bark, bite, scratch, claw, and growl.

❖ People need people...animals cannot substitute for the part that people play in the lives of humans.

❖ Do not become upset if people whom you spend a lot of time with and whose company you enjoy do not become your friends or do not establish lasting relationships. Sometimes people are just passing through your life at a specific time and for a specific purpose.

❖ When people indicate that they want to move on....let them go.

- ❖ When a relationship can no longer fulfill basic needs or the needs of someone else…let it go.
- ❖ There are good people and bad people…depends on what you consider to be good and bad.
- ❖ There will always be people to help you get through your pain…God will provide them.
- ❖ People who have found people to share their cherished moments and deepest pains have found friends.

Two are better than one; because they have a good reward for their labour.
For if they fall, the one will lift up his fellow: but woe to him that is alone when he falleth; for he hath not another to help him up. Ecclesiastes 4: 9-10

CHAPTER 16

Faith

Every Christian goes through trials. At these times it is natural to call on Jesus.

- ❖ Faith in God is very personal. It is something that has to have developed over time. You can't just suddenly trust someone with whom you have never had a relationship.

- ❖ Faith can be severely tested by individuals who question your actions.

- ❖ Faith is proved by testing. When I walked into the new house I found that the colors were the same as the house I was about to lose. There were many other aspect of the house which could not be seen from the outside which made it suitable to continue with my tutoring program. I would not have been sure what God had in store for me, if I had not obeyed the voice of God.

- ❖ Faith in God empowers you to act with conviction.

- ❖ Faith in God allows you to smile even when the storms of life are frenzied and continue to rage beyond what you think you can endure.

- ❖ Faith in God gives you patience to wait for the winds of destruction to subside.

- ❖ Faith in God says "Hold on" because God is with you all the way.

- ❖ Faith in God makes you stronger with each test.

- ❖ Faith in God maintains your sanity and takes away all fear.

- ❖ Faith is the opposite of fear.

❖ Faith in God encourages you to pray and read His Word.

Hearken, my beloved brethren, Hath not God chosen the poor of this world rich in faith, and heirs of the kingdom which he hath promised to them that love him? James 2:5

CHAPTER 17

Success

It has been said that "success is the best revenge". That might mean something if you are seeking revenge. Most times when people feel lost or alone, they are not really trying to get revenge. They are just trying to make it. If you believe the tragedies that you faced are because of what is done to you; then you may be thinking about revenge. That was not my case. Through all the pain, hurt and loneliness, I had a confidence that I would make it. That confidence was given to me by none other than God himself. He never left me. He kept me sane and He gave me His peace. I therefore had a successful year. I continued my tutoring service and had a great graduation ceremony. I lost two students at the end of the year, only because one went on to high school and the other because of relocation to another state. I gained another student however so I was back at my original number. I had promised a parent that for middle school she would not have to pay the school fees. Despite all I had gone through I was still able to keep that promise. I found new friends, joined a choir - the prestigious Alumni Singers and became a part of a walking group. Yes, I had had a successful year.

Many people judge success by what you own. But the Bible tells us in Luke 12:15 that *a man's life consisteth not in the abundance of the things which he possesses.* We live and we dream of all that we want, but many times those dreams are not to be realized. We covet what others have but we have no idea what it cost those people to achieve that which seems enviable. When we put our lives in God's hands, He decides what course it will take. If we remain faithful we will achieve success.

For the most part, the world's view of success is to drive a nice car, have beautiful children who are doing well in school or college, have a nice house, and a good job. If these things are not all properly lined up then we feel that we must fix it so that it appears that way.

I can't help thinking of my mother as I think of success. At her funeral I had the opportunity of writing the Remembrances. It was easy to write because her life was unique.. She was a simple woman, uneducated but intelligent, and filled with integrity, kindness, and a desire to serve God. At her funeral, strangers and friends alike asked me for copies of the Remembrances.

The inscription on her tombstone reads "She gave so much and asked for so little".

My mother who in life might be considered unimportant; in death was thought to be a dignitary. In fact one of my siblings overheard an onlooker ask "Which dignitary, [statesperson] has died?" My mother had not died tragically. This was not her present church…it was the church of her youth. Yet her funeral was attended by hundreds.

If judged by the world's standards perhaps her life would not be seen as a success. Yet her legacy is in my opinion, greater than any riches that many have left for their children. Love, respect, integrity, compassion, kindness, and going the extra mile were the hallmarks of her life. If by her life she has a home in heaven…that is success. If by her life on this earth…she is remembered fondly by family friends and those with whom she worked, that is success. So what now is my view of success?

❖ Success is relative. Since our lives have several aspects such as physical, academic, social, spiritual, financial, and others, an individual may be successful in one or more areas but an abysmal failure in other areas.

❖ Success is subjective. It is evident that many people look up to individuals who are financially successful even though their entire lifestyle may be quite questionable in the eyes of the law, the church or their family.

❖ Success does not always bring happiness. Many people who are envied for their fame and fortune are often lonely, unhappy and suicidal.

❖ Success is personal. Many individuals know what their goals are in life. If they have the desire and determination to achieve their goals; then they will become the person they wish to be and hence will know success.

❖ Success is a journey. It is a quest for an individual to achieve their dreams. This is perhaps why it does not always mean happiness.

❖ Success is transient. The world is temporal and so what may have meant a lot yesterday doesn't today.

❖ Success for the Christian is permanent. It is personal and rooted in Jesus Christ; it is the journey of life; it is fighting the wiles of the enemy; it does not always bring happiness, because God's desires for a Christian are totally unlike man's desires. It is only relative to Jesus Christ and the life He lived.

❖ Success in Christ is complete and total. The peace and joy we find when we trust in God, gives us a feeling of well-being which the world cannot understand.

❖ A successful man in the world's eyes; should not be poor, should not be humble; should not be without a host of friends; should not spend his life giving; should not travel miles to support a dead friend; should not eat with the poor; walk with the lowly; speak with prostitutes; be rejected by his friends; be jeered by many or die poor and alone. When Christ walked on this earth, this was His experience, and surely Christ was successful. He completed His mission and God the Father was well pleased with Him.

❖ When we walk with Christ our success is often questionable. He promised that we would suffer much the same fate as He did. He promised that we would be misunderstood, forsaken, disliked, accused, ridiculed and persecuted. *You will be hated by all because of My name, but it is the one who has endured to the end who will be saved* . Matthew 10:22.

❖ As a Christian, your legacy may not be as that of one who has gained much in the world, but of one who has given much.

❖ You may not be remembered for the many proud moments you had; but for the many moments that others achieved honor and greatness because of your sacrifice.

❖ You may not be remembered for all the books you wrote; but for the many books that you were instrumental in helping others to read.

❖ You may not be remembered for the wealth that you have accumulated; but for the wealth of joy that you brought to the life of others.

❖ Success for a Christian, is a legacy of love, joy, hope and peace. This is the legacy which every Christian should hope to have. This is the legacy of a life that truly mirrors that of Jesus Christ.

❖ Success for the Christian is a place in heaven.

CHAPTER 18

Final Thoughts

Much has happened since I decided to write this book. Sometimes I just could not motivate myself to write. Many times I was too busy.

When I was putting things in perspective, it suddenly occurred to me that all I had really lost was a house. It wasn't an appendage or an organ or a family member or a friend. It wasn't my integrity or my freedom. It was really just a house. We need to put things in perspective. Worrying and fretting about an outcome does not change the situation. Losing my house was indeed quite traumatic, but it was not something that was life threatening.

The minute I decided to put my trust in God and totally depend on him to lead me through the abyss of uncertainty, I was marked for victory. Satan was not going to be victorious. The taunts of the enemy became fainter and fainter. Hope took over from despair; joy took over sadness; love took over from hate; comfort took over from anguish; forgiveness took over from anger; strength took over from weakness; and loneliness gave way to companionship. My life became the antithesis of everything the enemy was intending.

Because I am a child of God, I am a natural target for attacks from the enemy. When I lost my house, he wanted to destroy me. He used every opportunity to destroy my joy, my peace, my hope my confidence, my relationship with my family, and render me unfit to live. It is the eternal warfare. So when we put things in perspective we should not hate the people around who seemed to have abandoned us, or ignored us, or talked about us; they are just pawns of the devil. They should know better perhaps, but has there ever been a time when I should have known better? Was there ever a time when I succumbed to the wiles of the devil? I certainly have! But what does the Bible say?

Therefore all things whatsoever ye would that men should do to you, do ye even so to them: for this is the law and the prophets. Matthew 7: 12

…not rendering evil for evil, or railing for railing: but contrariwise blessing; knowing that ye are thereunto called, that ye should inherit a blessing." 1Peter 3:9

But I say unto you, Love your enemies, bless them that curse you, do good to them that hate you, and pray for

them which despitefully use you, and persecute you
Matthew 5:44

Let all bitterness, and wrath, and anger, and clamor, and evil speaking, be put away from you, with all malice. Ephesians 4:31

This was really my test to pass or fail. I still second guess myself. The devil continually places people in my life who ask questions to make me question my decisions. I constantly retrace everything that happened leading up to the foreclosure and in the months and even the years following, and I am convinced that my actions were spirit-led.

You may question that. After all I lost my home and I used up my savings and pension. However what did I gain? I learned to trust in God. I really learned intellectually and experientially that you can totally trust in

God's promises and expect to be successful. I made new friends. I gained my life back. I have a new strength born out of the knowledge that God's love and mercy is unequivocally real. This gift of love, mercy and grace of which I speak is free to all, and when you have it; you have everything you need and hope to have in this life

For I know the thoughts that I think toward you, saith the LORD, thoughts of peace, and not of evil, to give you an expected end.

Then shall ye call upon me, and ye shall go and pray unto me, and I will hearken unto you.

And ye shall seek me, and find me, when ye shall search for me with all your heart. Jer. 29 11-13

My prayer for you dear reader is that if you are facing any kind of problems or foreclosure; if anything you cherish is being withdrawn, house, family, friends, job, life,

Just *"cast your cares on Him because He cares for you"*, 1Peter 5:7. He will reward your faith in Him with the joy, peace, strength, and the comfort you need to take you through. If you do not know my Jesus, I wish you will try Him today. Just ask Him to come into your life and forgive you of all your sins. When you do He will lead you to the next step.

Blessings and peace

Epilogue

This book has been five years in the making. It is very easy in a moment of pain or distress to write thoughts which match emotions but which lose the essence of the message. Although the book was written in perhaps a few months, it was revisited several times over the five years to make changes which support my spiritual growth.

The message has not been changed. I sincerely believe all that has been shared. I know as a fact that family is important, true friendship is priceless, success is relative, and that God never fails. In fact the years have only solidified the lessons learned. Life will always have storms, but there is a God the creator of the universe, who loves us so much that He will never leave us no matter what. *For I the Lord thy God will hold thy right hand, saying unto thee, Fear not; I will help thee*, Isaiah 41:13.

ABOUT THE AUTHOR

 Pauline Salmon is a Jamaican born educator who now resides in St. Petersburg, Florida. She holds a doctorate and a Masters degree in Education Leadership from Argosy University and a Bachelors of Arts degree from the University of the West Indies. Though an educator for over thirty years, her greatest passion is to share her love for Christ and her unwavering faith in God with others. Besides teaching, she writes plays and poems especially for church and is the CEO of a tutoring service since 1998. She believes that justice, honesty, and excellence should be the hallmark of all activities.

Cover design by Rupert Salmon and Ariana Salmon

42706678R00077

Made in the USA
Charleston, SC
06 June 2015